RAG PROGRAM

I0018031

THE DEFINITIVE GUIDE FOR ADVANCED PRACTITIONERS

LIAM HENRY JR

TABLE OF CONTENTS

Preface for RAG Programming: The Definitive Guide for Advanced Practitioners

The landscape of natural language processing (NLP) has undergone a dramatic transformation with the advent of large language models (LLMs). These models, capable of generating human-quality text, have opened up new possibilities for a wide range of applications. However, their potential is often limited by their reliance on static knowledge.

Retrieval-Augmented Generation (RAG) emerges as a powerful paradigm to bridge this gap. By combining the strengths of information retrieval and generative models, RAG systems can access and leverage vast amounts of external knowledge to produce more informative, relevant, and factually accurate outputs.

This book is designed to serve as a comprehensive guide for experienced practitioners seeking to master the intricacies of RAG programming. Our aim is to provide a deep dive into the theoretical underpinnings, practical implementation techniques, and advanced applications of RAG.

Whether you are a seasoned NLP researcher, a data scientist looking to build intelligent systems, or a software engineer aiming to develop innovative RAG-powered products, this book offers valuable insights and hands-on guidance. We explore the latest advancements in the field, address critical challenges, and provide practical strategies for building robust and effective RAG systems.

We believe that RAG has the potential to revolutionize the way we interact with information and generate content. Our hope is that this book will empower you to harness the full potential of this groundbreaking technology.

Chapter 1: Introduction to RAG Programming

1.1 What is RAG?

Retrieval-Augmented Generation (RAG) is a paradigm in natural language processing (NLP) that combines the strengths of information retrieval and generative models to produce improved text outputs. Unlike traditional language models that rely solely on their training data, RAG systems can access and leverage external knowledge sources to generate more informative, relevant, and factually accurate responses.

Core Components of a RAG System

A typical RAG system consists of three main components:

Retriever: This component is responsible for fetching relevant information from external knowledge sources in response to a given query. It employs techniques like keyword search, semantic search, or dense retrieval to identify and rank potential documents.

Generator: A language model, such as GPT-3, is used to generate text based on the provided query and retrieved information. The generator aims to create coherent and informative outputs while incorporating the relevant facts from the retrieved documents.

Knowledge Base: This component stores the external information that the RAG system can access. It can be a collection of documents, a database, or a knowledge graph.

By combining these components, RAG systems can effectively address the limitations of traditional language models and produce more comprehensive and informative outputs.

Retrieval-Augmented Generation (RAG)

Retrieval-Augmented Generation (RAG) is a technique that combines the power of information retrieval and generative AI to create more informative and accurate text outputs. It addresses the limitations of traditional language models by allowing them to access and incorporate external knowledge sources.

Essentially, RAG works by:

Retrieving relevant information: Given a user query, a retrieval system fetches pertinent documents or information from an external knowledge base.

Generating text: A language model then processes the retrieved information along with the original query to produce a comprehensive and informative response.

By augmenting the generation process with external knowledge, RAG systems can provide more accurate, up-to-date, and contextually relevant answers compared to traditional language models.

RAG vs. Traditional NLP and LLM-based Approaches

Traditional NLP

Traditional NLP techniques focus on analyzing and understanding human language through statistical methods and rule-based systems. They excel at tasks like:

Text classification: Categorizing text into predefined classes (e.g., sentiment analysis, spam detection).

Named entity recognition (NER): Identifying named entities in text (e.g., persons, organizations, locations).

Part-of-speech tagging: Assigning grammatical tags to words (e.g., noun, verb, adjective).

While effective for specific tasks, traditional NLP methods often struggle with complex language understanding and generation, especially in open-ended or ambiguous contexts.

LLM-based Approaches

Large Language Models (LLMs) have revolutionized NLP by leveraging deep learning to generate human-quality text. They are trained on massive amounts of text data and can perform tasks such as:

Text generation: Creating different text formats (articles, code, scripts, etc.)

Machine translation: Translating text from one language to another.

Summarization: Condensing long documents into shorter summaries.

However, LLMs suffer from several limitations:

Factuality: They can generate plausible but incorrect information.

Lack of grounding: They rely solely on the training data and may struggle with out-of-distribution queries.

Computational cost: Training and inference of LLMs can be computationally expensive.

RAG as a Differentiator

RAG addresses the shortcomings of both traditional NLP and LLM-based approaches by combining their strengths:

Access to external knowledge: RAG leverages information retrieval techniques to access relevant information from external sources, unlike traditional NLP and LLMs which are limited to their training data.

Improved accuracy and factuality: By grounding responses in factual information, RAG can produce more accurate and reliable outputs compared to LLMs alone.

Enhanced flexibility: RAG can adapt to different domains and tasks by incorporating diverse knowledge sources, offering greater flexibility than traditional NLP methods.

Improved coherence and relevance: RAG can generate more coherent and relevant text by combining the strengths of information retrieval and generation.

In essence, RAG represents a significant advancement in NLP by bridging the gap between information retrieval and language generation, leading to more informative and reliable systems.

Core Components of a RAG System

1. Retriever

The retriever is the first component of a RAG system responsible for fetching relevant information from an external knowledge base in response to a given query. It acts as a search engine within the system.

Key functions:

Identifying relevant documents or passages from the knowledge base based on the query.

Ranking the retrieved information based on relevance scores.

Returning a set of top-ranked documents to the generator.

Techniques:

Keyword-based search

Semantic search

Dense retrieval (using embeddings)

2. Generator

The generator is the second component that takes the retrieved information and the original query as input to produce a comprehensive and informative response.

Key functions:

Processing the retrieved information and the query.

Generating text that incorporates the relevant facts from the retrieved documents.

Ensuring coherence and fluency in the generated text.

Models:

Large Language Models (LLMs) like GPT-3, Jurassic-1 Jumbo

Sequence-to-sequence models

3. Knowledge Base

The knowledge base serves as the repository of information that the RAG system can access. It contains the data that the retriever searches through to find relevant information.

Types of knowledge bases:

Document collections (e.g., articles, reports)

Databases (e.g., structured data)

Knowledge graphs (structured representation of knowledge)

Key considerations:

Quality and relevance of information

Efficiency of search and retrieval

Size and scalability of the knowledge base

By effectively combining these three components, a RAG system can produce more informative, accurate, and relevant outputs compared to traditional language models.

Key Benefits of RAG

RAG offers several advantages over traditional NLP and LLM-based approaches:

Improved Accuracy

Factual grounding: By accessing and incorporating external knowledge, RAG systems can produce responses that are more aligned with real-world facts.

Reduced hallucinations: RAG helps to mitigate the issue of LLMs generating plausible but incorrect information.

Enhanced Factuality

Access to up-to-date information: RAG systems can access and process the latest information, ensuring that the generated text is based on current knowledge.

Verifiable claims: RAG can provide citations or references to support the information presented in the generated text, increasing credibility.

Increased Relevance

Contextual understanding: RAG systems can better understand the context of a query by accessing relevant information, leading to more relevant responses.

Tailored information: RAG can provide more specific and tailored information based on the user's query and the available knowledge.

By leveraging the strengths of both information retrieval and generative models, RAG systems can deliver significantly improved performance in various NLP tasks.

1.2 The Evolution of RAG

From Information Retrieval to RAG

The foundation of RAG lies in the field of information retrieval (IR). Traditional IR systems focused on retrieving relevant documents based on keyword matching or statistical models. However, these systems often struggled with semantic understanding and context.

The Role of Knowledge Graphs

Early attempts to enhance information retrieval involved the incorporation of knowledge graphs. These structured representations of knowledge provided a richer context for understanding and processing information. However, generating human-quality text from knowledge graphs remained a challenge.

The Emergence of LLMs

The advent of Large Language Models (LLMs) marked a significant turning point. LLMs demonstrated remarkable capabilities in generating human-quality text, but they suffered from limitations such as hallucination and lack of factual grounding.

The Integration of Retrieval and Generation

RAG emerged as a response to these challenges. By combining the strengths of information retrieval and LLMs, RAG systems could access and leverage external knowledge to produce more informative and accurate text outputs. This integration led to a paradigm shift in NLP, enabling the creation of more sophisticated and versatile language models.

Key Milestones and Advancements

Early RAG systems: Focused on simple keyword-based retrieval and rule-based generation.

Incorporation of semantic search: Improved retrieval accuracy by considering the meaning of words and phrases.

Leveraging dense embeddings: Enhanced semantic similarity between queries and documents.

Integration of advanced LLMs: Improved text generation quality and coherence.

Hybrid approaches: Combining different retrieval and generation techniques for optimal performance.

Brief Overview of Information Retrieval and Text Generation Techniques

Information Retrieval (IR)

Information Retrieval is the process of finding and retrieving relevant information from a collection of documents. It involves:

Indexing: Creating a structured representation of documents for efficient search.

Query processing: Transforming user queries into a form that can be matched against the index.

Ranking: Determining the relevance of documents to a query and presenting them in order of decreasing relevance.

Key techniques:

Boolean search: Using logical operators (AND, OR, NOT) to combine search terms.

Vector space model: Representing documents and queries as vectors in a high-dimensional space.

Probabilistic models: Estimating the probability of a document being relevant to a query.

Language modeling: Representing documents and queries as probability distributions over words.

Text Generation

Text generation involves creating new text formats such as articles, code, scripts, emails, etc. It has evolved significantly with advancements in machine learning.

Key techniques:

Template-based generation: Filling in predefined templates with relevant information.

Rule-based generation: Applying linguistic rules to create text.

Statistical machine translation: Treating text generation as a translation task.

Neural language models: Using deep learning models like Recurrent Neural Networks (RNNs), Long Short-Term Memory (LSTM), and Transformers to generate text.

These techniques have laid the foundation for the development of more sophisticated text generation models, including those used in RAG systems.

The Emergence of LLMs and Their Limitations

The Emergence of LLMs

Large Language Models (LLMs) have revolutionized the field of natural language processing (NLP) by leveraging deep learning to process and generate human-like text. These models are trained on massive amounts of text data, enabling them to learn complex patterns and generate coherent and contextually relevant text.

Key advancements that led to the emergence of LLMs include:

Transformer architecture: Introduced in the paper "Attention Is All You Need," the transformer architecture has become the backbone of most modern LLMs. It allows models to process input data in parallel, improving efficiency and accuracy.

Increased computational power: The availability of powerful GPUs and TPUs has made it possible to train larger and more complex models.

Massive datasets: The growth of digital text data has provided LLMs with ample training material.

Limitations of LLMs

Despite their impressive capabilities, LLMs have several limitations:

Factuality: LLMs can generate text that sounds plausible but is factually incorrect or misleading. This is often referred to as "hallucination."

Bias: LLMs can perpetuate biases present in their training data, leading to unfair or discriminatory outputs.

Lack of common sense: LLMs often struggle with tasks requiring real-world knowledge or common sense reasoning.

Computational cost: Training and running large LLMs requires significant computational resources.

Interpretability: The inner workings of LLMs are complex and difficult to understand, making it challenging to explain their decisions.

These limitations highlight the need for further research and development to address these challenges and unlock the full potential of LLMs.

The Role of Knowledge Graphs in Early RAG Systems

Knowledge graphs played a crucial role in the evolution of RAG systems, providing a structured representation of information that enhanced the capabilities of early retrieval and generation models.

Key Roles of Knowledge Graphs in Early RAG:

Structured Knowledge Base: Knowledge graphs served as a structured repository of factual information, providing a foundation for retrieval systems to access and process data efficiently.

Semantic Enrichment: By representing entities and their relationships, knowledge graphs enriched the understanding of query intent and document relevance, improving retrieval accuracy.

Factual Grounding: Knowledge graphs provided a ground truth for generated text, helping to mitigate the hallucination problem often associated with early language models.

Query Expansion: By leveraging semantic relationships between entities, knowledge graphs could be used to expand queries, leading to more comprehensive retrieval results.

Inference and Reasoning: While limited in early RAG systems, knowledge graphs laid the groundwork for more complex reasoning capabilities, enabling systems to infer new information based on existing knowledge.

While knowledge graphs were instrumental in advancing RAG, their limitations, such as the challenges in creating and maintaining large-scale knowledge bases, paved the way for the exploration of alternative approaches, including the use of dense embeddings and large language models.

The Impact of Transformer-Based Models on RAG

Transformer-based models have revolutionized the field of natural language processing, and their impact on RAG systems has been profound.

Key Impacts:

Enhanced Generation Capabilities: Transformers excel at generating human-quality text, making them ideal for the generation component of RAG systems. Their ability to capture long-range dependencies and contextual understanding significantly improves the coherence and relevance of generated outputs.

Improved Retrieval Effectiveness: Transformers can be used to create dense embeddings for both queries and documents, enabling more accurate and efficient semantic search. This leads to better retrieval of relevant information, which is crucial for the overall performance of RAG systems.

End-to-End RAG Systems: The versatility of transformers has made it possible to develop end-to-end RAG systems where the entire process, from retrieval to generation, is handled by a single transformer model. This simplifies the architecture and potentially improves performance.

Efficient Fine-Tuning: Transformers can be efficiently fine-tuned on specific datasets, enabling the adaptation of RAG systems to different domains and tasks. This flexibility is essential for building specialized RAG applications.

Specific Examples:

BERT and RoBERTa: These transformer-based models have been widely used for creating dense embeddings for documents and queries, improving retrieval accuracy.

GPT-3 and its successors: These powerful language models have demonstrated exceptional capabilities in text generation, making them popular choices for the generator component of RAG systems.

T5: This transformer-based model can be used for both retrieval and generation, enabling the development of end-to-end RAG systems.

By leveraging the strengths of transformer-based models, RAG systems have achieved significant advancements in terms of accuracy, relevance, and efficiency.

1.3 RAG Architecture Overview

Pipeline vs. End-to-End RAG

RAG systems can be structured in two primary architectures: pipeline and end-to-end.

Pipeline Architecture:

Involves distinct modules for retrieval and generation.

The retriever processes the query and retrieves relevant documents.

The generator processes the retrieved documents and the original query to produce the final output.

This architecture offers modularity and flexibility but can suffer from suboptimal interaction between the retriever and generator.

End-to-End Architecture:

Treats the entire RAG system as a single model.

A unified architecture processes the query, retrieves information, and generates the output in a single pass.

This approach can potentially improve performance by optimizing the entire system jointly but can be more complex to train and deploy.

The Role of Embeddings in RAG Systems

Embeddings play a crucial role in modern RAG systems. They are numerical representations of text data that capture semantic and syntactic information.

Document Embeddings: These represent the content of documents in a vector space.

Query Embeddings: These represent the meaning of a query in the same vector space.

Similarity Calculation: By calculating the cosine similarity or other distance metrics between document and query embeddings, the retriever can efficiently identify relevant documents.

Hybrid Approaches

Hybrid architectures combine elements of both pipeline and end-to-end approaches to leverage the strengths of each. For example, a system might use a pipeline architecture for initial retrieval and then fine-tune an end-to-end model on the retrieved information.

Pipeline vs. End-to-End RAG Architectures

Pipeline Architecture

Think of a pipeline as a series of connected steps. In a RAG pipeline:

Retrieval: The system first searches for relevant information from a knowledge base based on the user's query.

Generation: The retrieved information is then fed into a language model to generate a response.

This approach is like an assembly line, where each step has a specific task.

End-to-End Architecture

Imagine a single machine performing all the tasks. In an end-to-end RAG system:

Unified Model: A single model handles both retrieval and generation.

Joint Optimization: The entire system is trained together to optimize both steps simultaneously.

This approach is more integrated and can potentially achieve better performance but is often more complex to build and train.

In essence:

Pipeline: Separate modules for retrieval and generation.

End-to-End: A single model handles both tasks.

Would you like to delve deeper into the advantages and disadvantages of each architecture?

The Role of Embeddings in RAG Systems

Embeddings are at the heart of modern RAG systems. They are numerical representations of text data that capture semantic and syntactic information. In the context of RAG, embeddings play a crucial role in both the retrieval and generation components.

Embeddings in Retrieval

Document Embeddings: Each document in the knowledge base is converted into a dense vector representation.

Query Embeddings: The user's query is also transformed into a vector.

Similarity Search: By calculating the similarity between the query embedding and document embeddings, the system can efficiently retrieve the most relevant documents.

Embeddings allow for semantic search, which is more robust than keyword-based search as it considers the underlying meaning of words and phrases.

Embeddings in Generation

Contextual Embeddings: Embeddings can be used to represent the context of a query or a document, providing additional information to the language model.

Control Codes: Embeddings can be incorporated as control codes to guide the generation process, such as specifying desired styles, tones, or lengths.

By representing text as numerical vectors, embeddings enable efficient computations and facilitate the integration of information retrieval and language generation components in RAG systems.

Hybrid RAG Approaches

While pipeline and end-to-end architectures offer distinct advantages, they also have limitations. To address these, hybrid RAG approaches combine elements of both to create more robust and flexible systems.

Hybrid RAG involves integrating multiple retrieval and generation techniques to optimize performance based on specific use cases and constraints. This approach leverages the strengths of different methods to create a more comprehensive solution.

Key characteristics of hybrid RAG:

Combination of retrieval techniques: Employing multiple retrieval methods (e.g., keyword search, semantic search, dense retrieval) to enhance information retrieval capabilities.

Integration of generation models: Utilizing different language models or model ensembles for text generation to improve output quality and diversity.

Adaptive strategies: Dynamically adjusting the RAG architecture based on query characteristics, system performance, or other factors.

Hybrid architectures: Combining pipeline and end-to-end components to create a flexible and efficient system.

By carefully selecting and combining components, hybrid RAG systems can achieve better accuracy, relevance, and efficiency compared to pure pipeline or end-to-end approaches.

Flow of Information in a RAG System

User Query -> Retriever -> Relevant Documents -> Generator -> Generated Response

Breakdown:

User Query: The process begins with a user inputting a query or question.

Retriever: The query is sent to the retriever, which searches through a knowledge base to find relevant information.

Relevant Documents: The retriever returns a set of documents that are most relevant to the query.

Generator: The generator takes the original query and the retrieved documents as input. It processes this information to generate a comprehensive and informative response.

Generated Response: The final output, a response to the user's query, is presented.

Additional components (optional):

Embedding Layer: Converts text (query and documents) into numerical representations (embeddings) for efficient comparison.

Ranking Module: Ranks the retrieved documents based on their relevance to the query.

Feedback Loop: Incorporates user feedback to improve future responses.

This diagram provides a simplified overview of the information flow in a RAG system. Real-world implementations often involve more complex architectures and additional components.

1.4 RAG Applications

RAG's ability to combine information retrieval and generation has opened up a vast array of potential applications across various industries.

Showcase diverse applications of RAG across different domains (e.g., customer service, healthcare, finance)

Customer Service:

Intelligent chatbots capable of providing accurate and up-to-date information to customers.

Personalized product recommendations based on customer history and preferences.

Efficient handling of customer inquiries and complaints.

Healthcare:

Medical question answering systems that provide reliable and evidence-based information.

Drug discovery and development through analysis of medical literature and research data.

Personalized treatment recommendations based on patient data and medical guidelines.

Finance:

Financial analysis and reporting through automated data processing and summarization.

Fraud detection and prevention by analyzing financial transactions and identifying anomalies.

Investment recommendations based on market trends and historical data.

Discuss potential use cases and benefits for each application

Customer Service: Improved customer satisfaction, reduced response times, increased efficiency.

Healthcare: Enhanced patient care, accelerated medical research, improved decision-making.

Finance: Increased accuracy and efficiency in financial analysis, reduced risk of fraud, improved investment performance.

Highlight the challenges and opportunities in specific industries

Customer Service: Maintaining data privacy and security, ensuring the quality and relevance of retrieved information.

Healthcare: Addressing ethical concerns related to patient data, ensuring the accuracy of medical information.

Finance: Compliance with regulations, managing large volumes of financial data, mitigating biases in models.

By exploring these diverse applications, we can gain a deeper understanding of RAG's potential impact on various industries and identify opportunities for further research and development.

Diverse Applications of RAG Across Different Domains

Customer Service

Intelligent Virtual Assistants: RAG-powered virtual assistants can provide comprehensive and informative responses to customer inquiries, going beyond simple FAQs.

Personalized Recommendations: By analyzing customer behavior and preferences, RAG can offer tailored product or service recommendations.

Sentiment Analysis: RAG can be used to analyze customer feedback, identifying trends and areas for improvement.

Issue Resolution: By combining knowledge bases and customer interactions, RAG can assist in troubleshooting common issues and escalating complex problems.

Healthcare

Medical Question Answering: RAG can provide accurate and up-to-date medical information to patients and healthcare professionals.

Drug Discovery: By analyzing vast amounts of biomedical literature, RAG can accelerate the drug discovery process.

Clinical Decision Support: RAG can support healthcare providers in making informed decisions by providing relevant clinical information.

Patient Record Summarization: RAG can generate concise and informative summaries of patient medical records.

Finance

Financial Analysis: RAG can analyze financial data, generate reports, and provide insights for investment decisions.

Fraud Detection: By identifying patterns in fraudulent activities, RAG can help prevent financial losses.

Risk Assessment: RAG can assess financial risks by analyzing market trends and economic indicators.

Customer Support: RAG-powered chatbots can provide financial advice and support to customers.

Additional Domains

Education: Personalized learning experiences, intelligent tutoring systems, automated content creation.

Legal: Contract analysis, legal research, document summarization.

Marketing: Content generation, market research, customer segmentation.

These are just a few examples of how RAG can be applied across different domains. The potential applications are vast and continue to expand as the technology advances.

Potential Use Cases and Benefits for RAG Applications

Customer Service

Use Cases:

Resolving customer inquiries efficiently and accurately.

Providing personalized product recommendations.

Handling customer complaints and feedback effectively.

Offering 24/7 customer support.

Benefits:

Improved customer satisfaction through faster response times.

Increased efficiency by automating routine tasks.

Deeper customer insights through analysis of interactions.

Cost reduction through reduced reliance on human agents.

Healthcare

Use Cases:

Providing medical information and answering patient questions.

Supporting medical research and drug discovery.

Assisting in clinical decision-making.

Generating patient summaries and reports.

Benefits:

Improved patient outcomes through better access to information.

Accelerated medical research and development.

Enhanced efficiency in healthcare operations.

Reduced medical errors through knowledge-based support.

Finance

Use Cases:

Financial analysis and reporting.

Fraud detection and prevention.

Investment research and recommendations.

Risk assessment and management.

Customer financial advice.

Benefits:

Increased accuracy and speed in financial analysis.

Enhanced fraud prevention capabilities.

Improved investment returns through data-driven insights.

Better risk management through early identification of potential threats.

Improved customer satisfaction through personalized financial advice.

These are just a few examples of potential use cases and benefits for RAG applications in different domains. The specific applications and benefits will vary depending on the industry and the specific needs of the organization.

Challenges and Opportunities in Specific Industries

Customer Service

Challenges:

Ensuring data privacy and security of customer information.

Maintaining the quality and relevance of knowledge bases.

Overcoming limitations of natural language understanding.

Balancing automation with human interaction.

Opportunities:

Enhanced customer satisfaction through personalized experiences.

Increased operational efficiency and cost reduction.

New revenue streams through upselling and cross-selling.

Deeper customer insights for product improvement.

Healthcare

Challenges:

Ensuring data privacy and security of patient information.

Maintaining accuracy and reliability of medical information.

Addressing ethical concerns related to AI in healthcare.

Obtaining necessary regulatory approvals.

Opportunities:

Improved patient outcomes through personalized treatment plans.

Accelerated drug discovery and development.

Enhanced medical research through data analysis.

Increased access to healthcare services through remote consultations.

Finance

Challenges:

Compliance with financial regulations and data privacy laws.

Managing the complexity of financial data.

Preventing bias in AI models.

Ensuring the security of financial information.

Opportunities:

Improved fraud detection and prevention.

Enhanced risk assessment and management.

Personalized financial advice and recommendations.

Increased efficiency in financial operations.

These challenges and opportunities are not exhaustive and may vary depending on the specific application and implementation of RAG technology. Addressing these challenges and leveraging the opportunities will be crucial for the successful adoption of RAG in these industries.

1.5 RAG vs. Traditional NLP Techniques

Traditional NLP Techniques

Traditional NLP techniques primarily rely on statistical methods, rule-based systems, and machine learning algorithms to process and understand human language. These methods have been extensively used for tasks such as:

Text classification

Named entity recognition

Sentiment analysis

Machine translation

While effective for specific tasks, traditional NLP methods often face challenges in handling complex language structures, ambiguity, and real-world context.

RAG as an Advance

RAG represents a significant advancement over traditional NLP techniques by combining the strengths of information retrieval and generative models. It addresses the limitations of traditional methods by:

Leveraging External Knowledge: RAG can access and incorporate information from external sources, expanding the scope of potential responses.

Improved Factuality: By grounding responses in factual information, RAG reduces the risk of generating hallucinations or incorrect information.

Enhanced Contextual Understanding: RAG can better understand the context of a query by considering relevant information, leading to more accurate and relevant responses.

Increased Flexibility: RAG can be adapted to various domains and tasks by incorporating different knowledge sources and generation models.

Key Differences

Data Reliance: Traditional NLP methods primarily rely on training data, while RAG leverages both training data and external knowledge sources.

Task Focus: Traditional NLP often focuses on specific tasks, while RAG is more versatile and can handle a wider range of language understanding and generation challenges.

Output Quality: RAG generally produces more informative and accurate outputs compared to traditional methods, especially when dealing with complex or ambiguous queries.

In summary, RAG represents a paradigm shift in NLP, offering significant advantages over traditional techniques. By combining information retrieval and generation, RAG has the potential to revolutionize how we interact with language and information.

RAG vs. Traditional NLP Approaches

Rule-Based Systems

Reliance on Hand-crafted Rules: Rule-based systems heavily depend on human experts to define explicit rules for language processing.

Limitations: These systems are often brittle, struggling with ambiguity and real-world variations in language.

RAG Advantage: RAG overcomes these limitations by learning patterns from data and adapting to new information.

Statistical Methods

Data-Driven Approach: Statistical methods rely on large amounts of data to identify patterns and relationships between words.

Limitations: These methods often lack interpretability and can be sensitive to data quality.

RAG Advantage: RAG combines statistical methods with knowledge-based approaches, improving accuracy and interpretability.

Machine Learning Approaches

Learning from Data: Machine learning approaches learn patterns from data without explicit programming.

Limitations: Traditional machine learning models often require significant feature engineering and can struggle with complex language structures.

RAG Advantage: RAG builds upon machine learning advancements, specifically deep learning, to create more sophisticated and effective models.

RAG as a Synthesis

RAG represents a synthesis of these traditional approaches:

Rule-Based Elements: Implicit rules are learned from data through the retrieval component.

Statistical Foundations: Statistical methods are employed for both retrieval and generation.

Machine Learning Powerhouse: Deep learning models drive the generation component.

By combining these elements, RAG overcomes the limitations of individual approaches, resulting in more robust and versatile language processing capabilities.

Strengths and Weaknesses of Different NLP Approaches

Rule-Based Systems

Strengths: Precise control over output, good for well-defined tasks, efficient for small-scale applications.

Weaknesses: Difficulty in handling ambiguity, lack of adaptability to new language patterns, time-consuming development.

Statistical Methods

Strengths: Ability to handle large amounts of data, good for probabilistic tasks like language modeling, adaptable to different domains.

Weaknesses: Often requires significant data preprocessing, can be sensitive to data quality, lack of interpretability.

Machine Learning Approaches

Strengths: High accuracy on complex tasks, ability to learn from data, adaptability to new data.

Weaknesses: Requires large amounts of data, can be computationally expensive, potential for overfitting.

RAG

Strengths: Combines strengths of retrieval and generation, improved accuracy and factuality, adaptability to various domains.

Weaknesses: Reliance on the quality of the knowledge base, potential for biases in the retrieved information, computational cost.

In summary, rule-based systems are precise but inflexible, statistical methods are data-driven but lack interpretability, and machine learning excels at complex tasks but requires large amounts of data. RAG offers a hybrid approach that leverages the strengths of these methods while mitigating their weaknesses.

RAG's Advantages in Complex and Dynamic Environments

RAG excels in complex and dynamic environments due to its ability to:

Adapt to Evolving Information: RAG systems can continuously update their knowledge base to reflect changes in the real world, ensuring that generated responses remain relevant and accurate.

Handle Ambiguity and Uncertainty: By accessing a wide range of information sources, RAG can better handle ambiguous queries and provide more comprehensive responses.

Manage Complex Queries: RAG can break down complex queries into smaller components, retrieve relevant information for each component, and then combine the results to generate a coherent response.

Provide Contextual Understanding: By considering the context of a query, RAG can deliver more relevant and informative responses.

Leverage Diverse Data Sources: RAG can integrate information from various sources, including structured data, unstructured text, and knowledge graphs, providing a comprehensive view of the world.

Handle Real-time Information: RAG can process and incorporate real-time data, enabling it to provide up-to-date and timely information.

These advantages make RAG particularly well-suited for applications in domains such as finance, healthcare, and customer service, where information is constantly changing and the ability to adapt is crucial.

Chapter 2: Theoretical Foundations

2.1 Retrieval Models

Basic Retrieval Models

Information Retrieval (IR) is the science of finding information relevant to a user's need and presenting it in an accessible format. Traditional IR models form the foundation for many modern retrieval systems.

Boolean Retrieval: This model is based on Boolean logic (AND, OR, NOT). Documents are represented as sets of terms, and queries are expressed as Boolean expressions. While simple, it often leads to overly restrictive or overly permissive results.

Vector Space Model (VSM): Documents and queries are represented as vectors in a high-dimensional space. The similarity between a document and a query is calculated based on the cosine of the angle between their vectors. This model is more flexible than Boolean retrieval but can be sensitive to term frequencies.

Probabilistic Retrieval: This model estimates the probability of a document being relevant to a query based on statistical information. It offers a more nuanced approach to ranking documents but requires extensive training data.

Modern Retrieval Techniques

Advances in natural language processing and machine learning have led to the development of more sophisticated retrieval techniques.

Semantic Search: This approach focuses on understanding the meaning of queries and documents, going beyond keyword matching. Techniques like word embeddings and semantic similarity measures are employed.

Dense Retrieval: This technique uses dense vectors to represent documents and queries, enabling efficient similarity calculations. It often leverages deep learning models to create high-quality embeddings.

Learning to Rank: This approach treats retrieval as a ranking problem, learning to predict the relevance of documents to a query using machine learning algorithms.

Embedding Techniques

Embeddings are numerical representations of text data that capture semantic and syntactic information. They are crucial for modern retrieval systems.

Word Embeddings: Represent individual words as dense vectors, capturing semantic and syntactic relationships.

Document Embeddings: Represent entire documents as dense vectors, enabling efficient similarity calculations.

Query Embeddings: Represent user queries as dense vectors to facilitate matching with document embeddings.

Evaluation Metrics

To measure the effectiveness of retrieval systems, several metrics are commonly used:

Precision: The proportion of retrieved documents that are relevant.

Recall: The proportion of relevant documents that are retrieved.

F1-score: The harmonic mean of precision and recall.

Normalized Discounted Cumulative Gain (NDCG): Considers the position of relevant documents in the ranking.

Mean Average Precision (MAP): Evaluates the overall performance of a retrieval system across multiple queries.

By understanding these retrieval models, embedding techniques, and evaluation metrics, we can build a strong foundation for understanding RAG systems.

2.2 Generation Models

Language Modeling

At the core of text generation is the concept of language modeling. A language model assigns probabilities to sequences of words. For instance, given a sequence of words "The quick brown fox," a language model can predict the likelihood of the next word being "jumps."

N-gram Models: Earlier language models relied on counting word frequencies and their co-occurrences within a fixed window size (n-grams).

Statistical Language Models: More sophisticated models, like those based on Markov chains, capture dependencies between words beyond fixed-length windows.

Sequence-to-Sequence Models

To generate text from input sequences (e.g., translating from one language to another or summarizing text), sequence-to-sequence models are employed.

Encoder-Decoder Architecture: These models consist of an encoder that processes the input sequence and a decoder that generates the output sequence.

Attention Mechanism: To capture long-range dependencies in the input sequence, attention mechanisms are incorporated.

Transformer Architecture

The transformer architecture has revolutionized natural language processing, including text generation.

Self-Attention: Unlike recurrent neural networks, transformers rely on self-attention to weigh the importance of different parts of the input sequence.

Encoder-Decoder Structure: Transformers maintain the encoder-decoder structure but use self-attention in both the encoder and decoder.

Positional Encoding: Since transformers do not inherently capture sequence order, positional encoding is added to provide information about the relative positions of words.

Generative Pre-trained Transformers (GPTs)

GPT models are a class of transformer-based language models trained on massive amounts of text data.

Unsupervised Pre-training: GPT models are pre-trained on a massive corpus of text to learn language patterns and representations.

Fine-tuning: For specific tasks, GPT models can be fine-tuned on smaller, task-specific datasets.

Text Generation: GPT models can generate text, translate languages, write different kinds of creative content, and answer your questions in an informative way.

2.3 Embedding Techniques

Embeddings are numerical representations of words, phrases, or documents that capture semantic and syntactic information. They are crucial for various NLP tasks, including information retrieval and generation.

Word Embeddings

Distributed Representations: Word embeddings represent words as dense vectors in a continuous space.

Techniques:

Word2Vec: Learns word similarities based on context in a large corpus of text.

GloVe: Combines global word-frequency statistics with local context information.

FastText: Represents words as n-grams of characters, improving out-of-vocabulary word handling.

Properties:

Semantic and syntactic relationships between words are captured in the vector space.

Analogical reasoning tasks (e.g., king - man + woman = queen) can be performed using vector arithmetic.

Sentence Embeddings

Challenges: Representing the meaning of entire sentences is more complex than representing individual words.

Techniques:

Averaging word embeddings: A simple but often effective approach.

Recurrent Neural Networks (RNNs) or Long Short-Term Memory (LSTM) networks: Capture sequential information in sentences.

Transformer-based models: Utilize attention mechanisms to capture complex sentence structures.

Applications: Sentence similarity, text classification, and semantic search.

Document Embeddings

Challenges: Representing the entire content of a document in a fixed-size vector.

Techniques:

Averaging sentence embeddings: Similar to sentence embeddings, but applied at the document level.

Document-level language models: Train language models specifically for document representation.

Hierarchical embeddings: Break down documents into sections or paragraphs and create hierarchical embeddings.

Applications: Document clustering, information retrieval, and recommendation systems.

Evaluation of Embeddings

Intrinsic Evaluation: Assess the quality of embeddings based on tasks like word similarity, analogy, and word clustering.

Extrinsic Evaluation: Evaluate embeddings based on their performance in downstream tasks like information retrieval, text classification, or machine translation.

Embeddings are fundamental to modern NLP systems, including RAG, as they provide a powerful way to represent and compare textual data.

2.4 Evaluation Metrics

Evaluating the performance of RAG systems requires a combination of metrics for both retrieval and generation components.

Retrieval Evaluation

Precision: Measures the proportion of retrieved documents that are relevant to the query.

Recall: Measures the proportion of relevant documents that are successfully retrieved.

F1-score: The harmonic mean of precision and recall, providing a balance between the two.

Mean Average Precision (MAP): Considers the order of retrieved documents, assigning higher weights to relevant documents appearing earlier in the list.

Normalized Discounted Cumulative Gain (NDCG): Incorporates the position of relevant documents in the ranked list, giving higher scores to documents ranked higher.

Generation Evaluation

BLEU (Bilingual Evaluation Understudy): Compares generated text to reference translations by calculating n-gram matches.

ROUGE (Recall-Oriented Understudy for Gisting Evaluation): Focuses on recall-based metrics, measuring the overlap between generated text and reference summaries.

METEOR (Metric for Evaluation of Translation with Explicit Ordering): Combines word-level matching, stemming, and synonymy to improve correlation with human judgments.

Human Evaluation: Involves human experts assessing the quality of generated text based on various criteria, such as fluency, coherence, and relevance.

Combined Evaluation

Evaluating the overall performance of a RAG system is challenging due to the interdependence of retrieval and generation components. Potential approaches include:

Pipeline Evaluation: Evaluating retrieval and generation separately using their respective metrics.

End-to-End Evaluation: Assessing the overall system performance based on the quality of the final generated text.

Hybrid Evaluation: Combining both pipeline and end-to-end evaluation to get a comprehensive view.

It's important to select appropriate metrics based on the specific goals of the RAG system and the evaluation criteria. Additionally, combining multiple metrics often provides a more comprehensive assessment of performance.

Chapter 3: RAG Architectures

3.1 Pipeline vs. End-to-End RAG

Pipeline Architecture

A pipeline architecture for RAG involves distinct modules for retrieval and generation.

Components:

Retriever: Responsible for fetching relevant information from a knowledge base based on the query.

Generator: Takes the retrieved information and the original query to produce the final output.

Process:

The user submits a query.

The retriever processes the query and retrieves relevant documents from the knowledge base.

The retrieved documents are passed to the generator.

The generator processes the documents and the original query to produce the final response.

Advantages:

Modularity: Allows for independent development and optimization of retrieval and generation components.

Flexibility: Enables the use of different retrieval and generation models.

Easier to understand and debug.

Disadvantages:

Potential suboptimal interaction between retrieval and generation.

Error propagation: Errors in the retrieval stage can impact the quality of the generated output.

End-to-End Architecture

In an end-to-end RAG architecture, the entire system is trained as a single model.

Components:

A unified model that handles both retrieval and generation.

Process:

The user submits a query.

The model processes the query and retrieves relevant information from its internal representation.

The model generates the final response based on the query and retrieved information.

Advantages:

Joint optimization of retrieval and generation for better overall performance.

Potential for improved coherence and fluency in the generated output.

Disadvantages:

Increased complexity in training and development.

Difficulty in interpreting and debugging the model.

Comparison

Feature	Pipeline	End-to-End
Modularity	High	Low
Flexibility	High	Low
Performance	Potentially lower due to suboptimal interaction	Potentially higher due to joint optimization
Complexity	Lower	Higher

In summary, pipeline architectures offer greater flexibility and modularity, while end-to-end architectures have the potential for better overall performance but are more complex to build and train. The choice between the two depends on specific requirements, available resources, and desired trade-offs.

Pipeline Approach

Python

```python
import pandas as pd

from sklearn.feature_extraction.text import TfidfVectorizer

from sklearn.metrics.pairwise import cosine_similarity

import transformers
```

```python
# Sample data (replace with your own)

documents = [

    "This is the first document.",

    "This is the second document.",

    "And the third document."

]


# Retrieval component

vectorizer = TfidfVectorizer()

tfidf_matrix                              =
vectorizer.fit_transform(documents)


def retrieve_documents(query):

  query_vec = vectorizer.transform([query])

    similarities  =  cosine_similarity(query_vec,
tfidf_matrix).flatten()

  indices = similarities.argsort()[::-1]

  return [documents[i] for i in indices]


# Generation component
```

```python
tokenizer = transformers.AutoTokenizer.from_pretrained("gpt2")

model = transformers.AutoModelForSeq2SeqLM.from_pretrained("gpt2")


def generate_text(query, retrieved_documents):

    prompt = f"{query} Based on the following information:\n{''.join(retrieved_documents)}"

    input_ids = tokenizer.encode(prompt, return_tensors="pt")

    output = model.generate(input_ids, max_length=100, num_beams=5, early_stopping=True)

    return tokenizer.decode(output[0], skip_special_tokens=True)


# Example usage

query = "What are the documents about?"

retrieved_docs = retrieve_documents(query)

generated_text = generate_text(query, retrieved_docs)

print(generated_text)
```

3.2 Hybrid Approaches

Hybrid RAG architectures combine elements of both pipeline and end-to-end approaches to leverage their strengths and mitigate their weaknesses.

Types of Hybrid Approaches

Cascaded Hybrid:

This approach involves a sequential application of retrieval and generation modules.

The retriever initially identifies relevant documents.

The generated text from the first pass can be used to refine the retrieval process in subsequent iterations.

This iterative approach can improve the quality of retrieved information and the generated output.

Joint Training Hybrid:

A single model is trained to perform both retrieval and generation.

However, the model architecture incorporates distinct components for retrieval and generation.

This approach allows for joint optimization of both tasks but can be complex to train.

Hybrid Model:

This approach combines elements of pipeline and end-to-end architectures within a single system.

For example, a pipeline architecture can be used for initial retrieval, followed by an end-to-end model for generation and refinement.

Benefits of Hybrid Approaches

Improved performance: By combining the strengths of pipeline and end-to-end architectures, hybrid approaches can achieve better overall performance.

Increased flexibility: Hybrid models can adapt to different use cases and data characteristics.

Enhanced robustness: By combining multiple techniques, hybrid approaches can be more resilient to challenges such as data sparsity or noise.

Challenges

Complexity: Designing and implementing hybrid systems can be more complex than pure pipeline or end-to-end approaches.

Hyperparameter tuning: Finding the optimal configuration for hybrid systems can be challenging.

Evaluation: Assessing the performance of hybrid systems requires careful consideration of evaluation metrics.

By carefully considering the specific requirements of a RAG application, hybrid approaches can offer significant advantages over pure pipeline or end-to-end architectures.

3.3 RAG Components and Interactions

Retrieval Component

Knowledge Base: The foundation of information retrieval, containing documents, facts, or structured data.

Types: Document collections, databases, knowledge graphs.

Indexing: Transforming knowledge base content into a searchable format for efficient retrieval.

Techniques: Inverted indexes, term frequency-inverse document frequency (TF-IDF), embeddings.

Query Processing: Converting user queries into a suitable format for retrieval.

Techniques: Natural language processing, query expansion, query rewriting.

Ranking: Determining the relevance of retrieved documents to the query.

Algorithms: BM25, language models, learning-to-rank.

Generation Component

Language Model: The core of text generation, capable of producing human-like text.

Types: Recurrent Neural Networks (RNNs), Long Short-Term Memory (LSTM), Transformers.

Decoding: Converting the internal representation of the language model into text output.

Techniques: Greedy decoding, beam search, nucleus sampling.

Prompt Engineering: Crafting effective prompts to guide the generation process.

Techniques: Template-based prompting, few-shot learning, chain-of-thought prompting.

Knowledge Base and Generation Interaction

Retrieval-Augmented Generation: The generator accesses retrieved documents to enrich the generated text.

Factuality and Relevance: The generator leverages information from the knowledge base to improve the accuracy and relevance of the output.

Knowledge Grounding: Aligning generated text with the factual content of the knowledge base.

Embedding Layer

Document Embeddings: Representing documents as dense vectors in a semantic space.

Query Embeddings: Representing user queries as dense vectors.

Similarity Search: Finding documents closest to the query based on embedding similarity.

Hybrid Embeddings: Combining different embedding techniques for improved performance.

Feedback Mechanisms

User Feedback: Incorporating user ratings, corrections, or preferences to refine the system.

Reinforcement Learning: Training the system to maximize rewards based on user interactions.

Iterative Refinement: Using generated text as input for further retrieval and generation cycles.

By understanding the interplay of these components, developers can build effective RAG systems that deliver high-quality outputs.

3.4 Challenges and Considerations

Building effective RAG systems presents several challenges that require careful consideration.

Efficiency

Computational Costs: Training and deploying large-scale RAG models can be computationally expensive.

Inference Latency: Ensuring fast response times for user queries is crucial.

Hardware and Software Optimization: Exploring techniques to optimize resource utilization.

Scalability

Handling Large Knowledge Bases: Efficiently indexing and searching through massive datasets.

Scaling RAG Systems: Expanding the system to handle increased query loads and data volumes.

Distributed Computing: Leveraging distributed architectures for scalability.

Ethical Considerations

Bias: Mitigating biases present in training data and models.

Fairness: Ensuring equitable treatment of different user groups.

Privacy: Protecting user data and preventing misuse of information.

Misinformation: Preventing the spread of false or misleading information.

Evaluation

Metric Selection: Choosing appropriate metrics to assess RAG system performance.

Human Evaluation: Incorporating human judgment to measure subjective aspects of quality.

Dynamic Evaluation: Developing evaluation methods for evolving systems.

Other Considerations

Knowledge Base Quality: Ensuring the accuracy and relevance of information in the knowledge base.

User Experience: Designing user interfaces that effectively interact with the RAG system.

Continuous Improvement: Implementing feedback mechanisms to refine the system over time.

Addressing these challenges is essential for building robust and reliable RAG systems.

Chapter 4: Building RAG Systems

This chapter will delve into the practical aspects of constructing a RAG system.

4.1 Data Preparation and Preprocessing

Data is the cornerstone of any successful RAG system. Effective data preparation and preprocessing are crucial for ensuring the quality and relevance of the information extracted.

Data Collection

Identifying Relevant Sources: Determining the appropriate data sources based on the target domain and application.

Data Acquisition: Gathering data from diverse sources, including text, structured data, and images.

Data Format: Converting data into a standardized format (e.g., JSON, CSV, XML).

Data Cleaning

Handling Missing Values: Imputing missing data or removing records with excessive missing values.

Noise Removal: Identifying and eliminating irrelevant or noisy information.

Data Consistency: Ensuring data uniformity and consistency across different sources.

Outlier Detection and Handling: Identifying and addressing abnormal data points.

Data Preprocessing

Tokenization: Breaking text into individual words or subwords.

Stop Word Removal: Eliminating common words that add little semantic value.

Stemming and Lemmatization: Reducing words to their root form for better representation.

Part-of-Speech Tagging: Assigning grammatical tags to words for further analysis.

Named Entity Recognition (NER): Identifying and classifying named entities (e.g., persons, organizations, locations).

Data Formatting

Structured Data: Converting unstructured text into structured formats (e.g., tables, databases).

Knowledge Graph Creation: Extracting entities and relationships to build a knowledge graph.

Data Indexing: Creating efficient indexes for fast retrieval.

By meticulously preparing and preprocessing data, we lay a solid foundation for building effective RAG systems.

Data Preparation and Preprocessing

```python
import pandas as pd

import numpy as np

from sklearn.feature_extraction.text import TfidfVectorizer

from nltk.tokenize import word_tokenize

from nltk.corpus import stopwords


# Sample data (replace with your own)

data = [

    "This is the first document.",

    "This is the second document.",

    "And the third document."

]


# Create a pandas DataFrame

df = pd.DataFrame({'text': data})


# Preprocessing

def preprocess(text):
```

```python
    # Tokenization

    tokens = word_tokenize(text.lower())

    # Remove stop words

    tokens = [word for word in tokens if word not
in stopwords.words('english')]

    return ' '.join(tokens)



df['processed_text']                                    =
df['text'].apply(preprocess)



# Create TF-IDF vectors

vectorizer = TfidfVectorizer()

tfidf_matrix                                            =
vectorizer.fit_transform(df['processed_text'])
```

4.2 Retrieval System Development

Knowledge Base Construction

Data Structures: Choosing appropriate data structures (e.g., inverted indexes, graphs) to store and organize information.

Data Indexing: Creating efficient indexes to speed up search operations.

Knowledge Graph Creation: Extracting entities and relationships to build a structured knowledge base.

Embedding Generation

Embedding Techniques: Selecting suitable embedding techniques (Word2Vec, GloVe, BERT, etc.) based on data characteristics and computational resources.

Embedding Generation Process: Creating embeddings for documents, queries, and entities.

Embedding Dimensionality: Determining the optimal embedding size for the target application.

Search Engine Implementation

Search Algorithms: Choosing appropriate search algorithms (e.g., Boolean, vector space, probabilistic, semantic search).

Index Construction: Building inverted indexes or other data structures to facilitate efficient search.

Query Processing: Transforming user queries into a searchable format.

Ranking Algorithms: Implementing ranking functions to order search results based on relevance.

Ranking Algorithms

Traditional Ranking: Using techniques like TF-IDF, BM25, and probabilistic models.

Learning-to-Rank: Training machine learning models to predict document relevance based on features.

Neural Ranking: Leveraging deep learning models for ranking, incorporating semantic and contextual information.

By carefully designing and implementing these components, an effective retrieval system can be built to support the RAG system.

Retrieval System Development

Python

```python
from sklearn.metrics.pairwise import cosine_similarity


def retrieve_documents(query):
    query_vec = vectorizer.transform([query])

    similarity_scores = cosine_similarity(query_vec,
    tfidf_matrix).flatten()

    top_indices = similarity_scores.argsort()[-5:][::-1]    # Retrieve top 5 documents

    return df.iloc[top_indices]['text'].tolist()


# Example usage

query = "what are the documents about"

retrieved_docs = retrieve_documents(query)

print(retrieved_docs)
```

4.3 Generation Model Fine-Tuning

Fine-tuning a pre-trained language model is crucial for adapting it to a specific RAG application. This process involves adjusting the model's parameters on a smaller, task-specific dataset.

Model Selection

Pre-trained Models: Choosing a suitable pre-trained model based on factors like model size, architecture, and domain relevance (e.g., BERT, GPT-3, RoBERTa).

Transfer Learning: Leveraging the knowledge acquired during pre-training to accelerate the fine-tuning process.

Data Preparation

Data Collection: Gathering relevant data for fine-tuning, ensuring it aligns with the target task.

Data Formatting: Converting data into a format compatible with the chosen language model.

Data Augmentation: Increasing data diversity through techniques like back translation, synonym replacement, and text generation.

Fine-Tuning Process

Objective Function: Defining the loss function to optimize during training (e.g., cross-entropy loss for text generation).

Hyperparameter Tuning: Experimenting with different hyperparameters (learning rate, batch size, epochs) to find the optimal configuration.

Training Process: Iteratively updating model parameters based on the training data and loss function.

Evaluation: Assessing the model's performance on a validation set to monitor progress and prevent overfitting.

Evaluation

Metrics: Using appropriate metrics to evaluate the fine-tuned model (e.g., BLEU, ROUGE, perplexity).

Human Evaluation: Assessing the quality of generated text through human judgment.

By carefully selecting a pre-trained model and fine-tuning it on relevant data, we can create a generation model tailored to the specific needs of a RAG system.

Generation Model Fine-Tuning

Python

```python
import transformers


# Load a pre-trained model

model_name = "gpt2"

tokenizer =
transformers.AutoTokenizer.from_pretrained(model_
name)
```

```python
model                                    =
transformers.AutoModelForSeq2SeqLM.from_pretraine
d(model_name)


# Prepare training data (replace with your own)

training_data = [

    {"input_ids": tokenizer.encode("This is a
prompt"), "labels": tokenizer.encode("This is the
generated text")},

    # ... more training examples

]


# Fine-tune the model

trainer = transformers.Trainer(

    model=model,

    args=training_args,    # Define training
arguments like output_dir, num_train_epochs, etc.

    train_dataset=training_data,

    data_collator=lambda data: {

        'input_ids': [item['input_ids'] for item
in data],

        'labels': [item['labels'] for item in
data]
```

```
    },

    # Other trainer arguments

)

trainer.train()
```

4.4 Integration of Retrieval and Generation

Integrating retrieval and generation components to create a cohesive RAG system requires careful consideration.

Prompt Engineering

Effective Prompts: Crafting clear and informative prompts to guide the generation process.

Contextual Information: Incorporating relevant information from retrieved documents into the prompt.

Constraints and Guidelines: Providing specific instructions to the model (e.g., length, style, format).

Knowledge Incorporation

Document Summarization: Extracting key information from retrieved documents.

Fact Extraction: Identifying relevant facts and entities from the documents.

Knowledge Graph Integration: Leveraging knowledge graphs to structure and organize information.

Response Formatting

Structure: Organizing the generated text into a coherent and readable format.

Coherence: Ensuring smooth transitions between different parts of the response.

Factuality: Verifying the accuracy of the generated content against the retrieved information.

Relevance: Aligning the response with the original query and its context.

Challenges and Considerations

Prompt Engineering Challenges: Creating effective prompts can be challenging, especially for complex queries.

Knowledge Integration: Incorporating knowledge from multiple sources while maintaining coherence can be difficult.

Factuality Verification: Ensuring the accuracy of generated information is crucial but challenging.

Response Quality: Balancing fluency, informativeness, and coherence in the generated text.

By effectively integrating retrieval and generation, RAG systems can produce high-quality and informative responses to user queries.

Integration of Retrieval and Generation

Python

```python
def generate_response(query):
```

```
retrieved_docs = retrieve_documents(query)

    prompt = f"Query: {query}\nContext: {',
'.join(retrieved_docs)}"

    input_ids = tokenizer.encode(prompt,
return_tensors="pt")

    output = model.generate(input_ids,
max_length=100, num_beams=5, early_stopping=True)

    return tokenizer.decode(output[0],
skip_special_tokens=True)
```

4.5 System Evaluation

Evaluating the performance of a RAG system is crucial for identifying strengths, weaknesses, and areas for improvement. It involves a combination of automated metrics and human judgment.

Evaluation Metrics

Retrieval Metrics: Precision, recall, F1-score, MAP, NDCG to assess the effectiveness of the retrieval component.

Generation Metrics: BLEU, ROUGE, METEOR, perplexity to evaluate the quality of generated text.

Combined Metrics: Holistic metrics that consider both retrieval and generation, such as human judgment-based ratings.

Human Evaluation

Relevance: Assessing whether the generated response addresses the user's query.

Coherence: Evaluating the logical flow and consistency of the generated text.

Factuality: Determining the accuracy of information presented in the response.

Informativeness: Measuring the extent to which the response provides useful information.

Iterative Improvement

Feedback Loops: Incorporating user feedback to refine the system.

A/B Testing: Comparing different system configurations to identify improvements.

Continuous Monitoring: Tracking system performance over time to detect issues and trends.

Challenges

Subjectivity: Human evaluation can be subjective and inconsistent.

Metric Limitations: Existing metrics may not fully capture the nuances of RAG system performance.

Dynamic Evaluation: Assessing system performance in real-world, changing conditions.

By combining automated metrics and human evaluation, it's possible to obtain a comprehensive understanding of a RAG system's strengths and weaknesses.

Chapter 5: Advanced Topics

This chapter delves into more complex and specialized aspects of RAG systems, exploring cutting-edge research and potential future directions.

5.1 Evaluation Metrics and Challenges

Evaluating the performance of RAG systems is a complex task due to the interplay of retrieval and generation components. While traditional metrics can provide insights, they often fall short in capturing the nuances of RAG systems.

Challenges in RAG Evaluation

Combined Evaluation: Balancing the evaluation of retrieval and generation components.

Dynamic Nature: Accounting for the evolving nature of information and user queries.

Subjectivity: Incorporating human judgment to assess factors like relevance, coherence, and factuality.

Metric Limitations: Existing metrics may not fully capture the desired aspects of RAG performance.

Evaluation Metrics

Retrieval Metrics:

Precision, recall, F1-score, MAP, NDCG: These traditional metrics can be used to evaluate the effectiveness of the retrieval component.

Semantic similarity metrics: Measuring the semantic similarity between retrieved documents and the query.

Generation Metrics:

BLEU, ROUGE, METEOR: These metrics can assess the quality of generated text but may not fully capture the nuances of RAG outputs.

Human evaluation: Subjective ratings by human experts to assess relevance, coherence, and factuality.

Hybrid Metrics:

Combining retrieval and generation metrics to provide a more comprehensive evaluation.

User satisfaction metrics: Directly measuring user experience and preferences.

Advanced Evaluation Techniques

Task-Based Evaluation: Assessing the performance of the RAG system in specific tasks or scenarios.

Multidimensional Evaluation: Considering multiple aspects of system performance, such as efficiency, robustness, and explainability.

Continuous Evaluation: Monitoring system performance over time to detect changes and trends.

By carefully selecting and combining evaluation metrics, it is possible to gain valuable insights into the strengths and weaknesses of a RAG system.

5.2 RAG for Specific Domains

RAG systems can be tailored to excel in specific domains by adapting various components to the domain's unique characteristics.

Domain Adaptation

Data-Centric Approach: Collecting and preparing domain-specific data for training and fine-tuning.

Model Adaptation: Fine-tuning pre-trained models on domain-specific data to improve performance.

Knowledge Base Construction: Creating domain-specific knowledge bases or augmenting existing ones.

Domain-Specific Knowledge Bases

Structured Knowledge: Leveraging domain-specific ontologies and knowledge graphs.

Unstructured Data: Incorporating domain-specific text, documents, and multimedia.

Data Quality: Ensuring the accuracy, completeness, and consistency of domain-specific information.

Domain-Specific Evaluation Metrics

Task-Specific Metrics: Developing evaluation metrics aligned with domain-specific goals.

Human Expertise: Incorporating domain experts in the evaluation process.

Benchmark Datasets: Creating or utilizing domain-specific benchmark datasets for comparison.

Examples of Domain-Specific RAG Systems

Healthcare: Medical question answering, drug discovery, patient record summarization.

Finance: Financial analysis, investment recommendations, fraud detection.

Legal: Legal research, contract analysis, document summarization.

Customer Service: Intelligent chatbots, product recommendations, sentiment analysis.

By carefully considering domain-specific requirements, RAG systems can be optimized to deliver superior performance and value.

5.3 Ethical Considerations

Ethical considerations are paramount in the development and deployment of RAG systems. These systems must be designed and operated responsibly to avoid negative impacts.

Fairness and Bias

Bias in Data: Identifying and mitigating biases present in training data.

Fairness Metrics: Developing evaluation metrics to assess fairness and equity.

Bias Mitigation Techniques: Implementing strategies to reduce bias in models and outputs.

Privacy

Data Protection: Safeguarding user data and adhering to privacy regulations (e.g., GDPR, CCPA).

Data Minimization: Collecting and storing only necessary data.

Anonymization and Pseudonymization: Protecting user identity while preserving data utility.

Misinformation

Fact-Checking: Verifying information from reliable sources.

Contextual Understanding: Providing context for generated information to prevent misinterpretation.

Transparency: Disclosing the limitations of the system and the potential for errors.

Transparency and Explainability

Model Interpretability: Understanding the decision-making process of the model.

Feature Importance: Identifying the factors influencing the model's output.

User Communication: Clearly communicating the capabilities and limitations of the system.

Accountability

Responsible Development: Ensuring that RAG systems are developed and deployed ethically.

Error Correction: Implementing mechanisms to address errors and biases.

Continuous Monitoring: Regularly assessing the system's performance and impact.

By addressing these ethical considerations, developers can build RAG systems that are trustworthy, fair, and beneficial to society.

5.4 Future Directions

The field of RAG is rapidly evolving, with numerous opportunities for advancements and innovations.

Continual Learning

Adaptive Models: Developing RAG systems that can continuously learn and adapt to new information without extensive retraining.

Concept Drift: Addressing the challenge of evolving knowledge bases and user preferences.

Zero-Shot and Few-Shot Learning

Limited Data Scenarios: Enabling RAG systems to perform tasks with minimal or no labeled data.

Transfer Learning: Leveraging knowledge from related tasks to improve performance on new tasks.

Explainable RAG

Interpretability: Developing techniques to understand the reasoning behind RAG system decisions.

Transparency: Communicating the decision-making process to users in a clear and understandable manner.

Trustworthiness: Building user trust through explainability and accountability.

User Experience

Human-Centered Design: Designing RAG systems with a focus on user needs and preferences.

Multimodal Interactions: Incorporating different modalities (text, speech, images) for enhanced user experience.

Personalization: Tailoring RAG systems to individual users based on their preferences and behavior.

Other Emerging Areas

Multilingual RAG: Developing RAG systems capable of handling multiple languages.

RAG for Complex Question Answering: Addressing complex and open-ended questions.

RAG for Summarization and Abstracting: Generating concise and informative summaries of long documents.

By exploring these directions, researchers and developers can push the boundaries of RAG technology and create even more powerful and versatile systems.

www.ingramcontent.com/pod-product-compliance
Lightning Source LLC
LaVergne TN
LVHW051740050326
832903LV00023B/1029